Cutting & Pattern Tips:

 It's easiest to cut accurate strips, rectangles, squares and triangles by using a paper trimmer or a ruler and X-acto® knife. However, measuring and drawing lines is another method to use. Cut a strip to the desired width, then cut it crosswise into the lengths needed. Cut a square diagonally to make two right triangles.

To make other shapes, first trace the pattern from this book onto tracing paper (use a ruler to make sure the lines are straight). Cut it out.

For cutting photos, move a tracing paper pattern around over the photo to decide what area works best with the shape—you can see through the tracing paper to center the subject. Trace around the pattern with a pencil or permanent pen, then cut out the photo.

To make it easier to lay out multiple shapes economically on your paper, make several patterns of each shape. Use 2-way or repositionable glue on the back of the patterns; let dry. Arrange the patterns on the paper—the repositionable glue will keep them in place without damaging the paper. Cut around them, or trace with pencil and cut on the pencil lines. Remove the patterns.

To make the best use of your papers, organize your patterns on the paper before cutting. Place long or large shapes first. Turn triangles and diamonds in different directions to fit as many as possible together. Small shapes can be cut from inside photo mats or background pieces in areas that will not show when the page is assembled.

Cropping Tips:

When cropping photos with scissors, it's easier to hold the scissors in one position and move the photo as you cut along the traced lines.

When cropping away the unnecessary background, be sure to save historical features like a house, car or piece of furniture—they'll be fun to see years from now.

Matting Photos & Journaling Pieces:

First glue the cropped photo to the selected paper, then trim the paper ⅛"–½" away from the photo. Use either straight or pattern-edged scissors.

For another effect, double-mat or triple-mat some photos: Just glue the matted photo to another paper and trim again. Repeat as many times as you want! It's fun to mix straight and pattern-cut mats.

In paper quilting, sometimes the photos and mats are cut to a measured size before assembly. In that case just center each piece on the next larger one and glue in place.

border strip pattern for

Annalise

8 Months

(instructions on page 2)

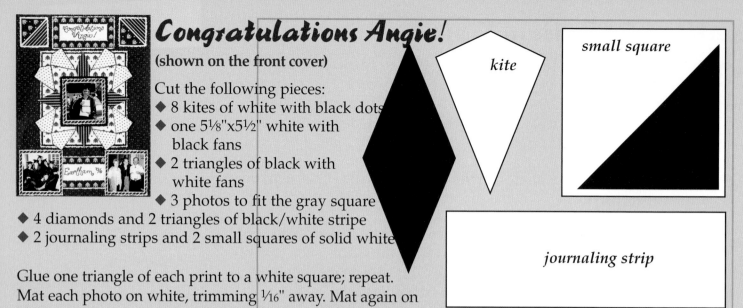

Congratulations Angie!

(shown on the front cover)

Cut the following pieces:
- 8 kites of white with black dots
- one 5⅛"x5½" white with black fans
- 2 triangles of black with white fans
- 3 photos to fit the gray square
- 4 diamonds and 2 triangles of black/white stripe
- 2 journaling strips and 2 small squares of solid white

kite

small square

journaling strip

Glue one triangle of each print to a white square; repeat. Mat each photo on white, trimming ¹⁄₁₆" away. Mat again on black/white stripe, trimming ⅛" away. Mat again on white, trimming ⅛" away. Journal on the white strips, then mat each on black with white fans, trimming ½" away. Mat again on white. Use decorative scissors to trim all these white mats. Mat each kite on black. Use straight scissors to trim very close to the edge, leaving a narrow black outline. Mat the 5⅛"x5½" piece on black, then on white, trimming each mat to ⅛" with patterned scissors. Mat the center photo again on black, trimming ⅛" away with patterned scissors.

Use the 8½"x11" black dotted sheet for the background. Glue a matted journaling strip ½" above the center bottom and the large square ½" above it. Glue the remaining journaling strip to the center top. Glue a photo square to each bottom corner, overlapping the journaling strip, and a triangle square to each upper corner. Arrange the diamonds and kites on the large square as shown and glue the center photo over them.

5⅛"x5½" piece

Annalise 8 Months **(shown on the front cover)**

- 12"x12" solid blue background sheet
- ¾" bow, ⅜" & ⅞" heart punches (McGill, Inc.)

Cut the following pieces:
- 4 border strips of pastel hearts (pattern on page 1); use patterned scissors
- 6 large squares of solid pink
- 3 medium squares of pastel dots on white
- 3 medium squares of pastel stripes on white
- 3 die-cut bears of pastel plaid
- 3 die-cut bears of pink tri-dot
- 3 photos to fit the small square

large square   *medium square*

small square

Glue the border strips vertically, evenly spaced across the background sheet with ½" on each side. Glue the bears to the outside strips, spaced as shown.

Layer a photo, a striped square and pink square. Repeat with the remaining photos. Glue the pastel dot squares to the remaining pink squares. Arrange them evenly spaced on the two center border strips, alternating photo squares with dot squares.

Decorate the page with punches and journaling as shown. Use a white opaque pen to outline the entire page and each border strip with a dashed line.

2

bear © & ™ Ellison® Craft & Design

35th Anniversary Party (shown on the front cover)

1³⁄₈"x3"
(cut 2 of border lace)

Cut the pieces as shown on the patterns. Also cut a 6½"x9" piece of solid purple.

Mat each square on solid purple and trim ⅛" away. Glue to the page corners, then mount the 6½"x9" piece centered on the page so it overlaps the squares.

Glue the photo to the center of the mat, then arrange and glue the remaining pieces on the 6½"x9" piece as shown, allowing room for journaling at the top and bottom. Journal with a white opaque pen.

1½"x1¾"
(cut 4 of floral)

photo mat (cut 1 of purple dot)

photo

1½"x2¼"
(cut 4 of lattice)

1½" square
(cut 4 of purple dot)

Our Engagement

(shown on the front cover)

◆ ³⁄₁₆" heart punch (Marvy® Uchida)
Cut the following pieces:
◆ 3 small octagons from lace paper
◆ 4 small octagons from swirl paper
◆ four 1" diamonds from tan tri-dot
◆ 4 rust and 4 black ½" diamonds
◆ 1 photo cut to fit the large octagon

Mat the photo on tan tri-dot; use patterned scissors to trim ¼" away. Mat again on rust, using straight scissors to trim ¹⁄₁₆" away, and a third time on black, using the patterned scissors to trim very close to the rust edge. Glue in the page center.

Mat each lace octagon on rust, using straight scissors to trim ¹⁄₁₆" away. Cut one in half vertically. Mat each swirl octagon and the 1" diamonds on black, trimming ¹⁄₁₆" away with patterned scissors.

Glue one lace and two swirl octagons above the photo as shown, with the center octagon overlapping the side ones. Repeat below the photo. Place a half octagon on each side, aligning the cut edges with the page edges. Glue the diamonds as shown. Journal with a white opaque pen.

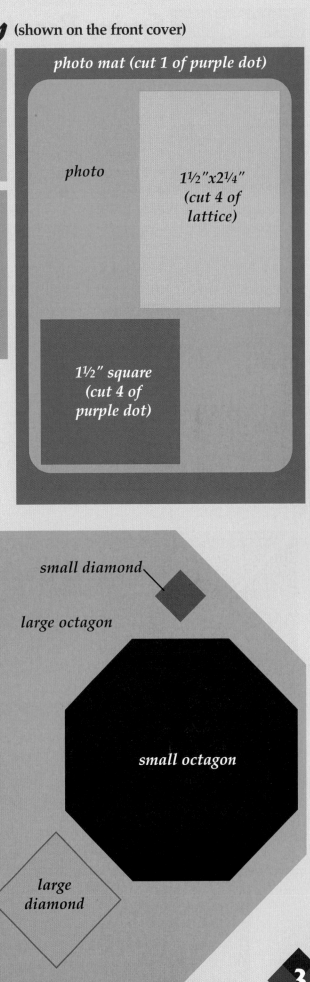

small diamond

large octagon

small octagon

large diamond

Spring Break '98 (shown on the front cover)

Cut the following pieces:
- ◆ 4 large squares of pink/black plaid (make sure the black area of the plaid borders the entire square)
- ◆ 2 small squares each of pink tri-dot, blue/black check, pink/blue diamonds and black with pink/blue stripes
- ◆ 2 large black squares
- ◆ 1 medium and 2 small diamonds of pink tri-dot
- ◆ 6 triangles of black with pink/blue stripes
- ◆ 2 trapezoids each of solid black and blue/black check
- ◆ 2 photos to fit the gray square photo pattern and 1 photo to fit the gray diamond photo pattern

Glue a black, then a blue trapezoid to the top edge of the page. Fill the notches on each end with a triangle and in the center with a small diamond. Repeat along the bottom. Glue one remaining triangle midway along each side.

Glue the small photo to the center of the large pink diamond. Glue the remaining photos to the black squares. Mat each small square on solid black, trimming 1/16" away.

Turn the pink plaid squares on point to form diamonds. Place the photo diamond in the page center and arrange the plaid diamonds around it as shown. Glue a matted photo to the top right and bottom left diamond. Glue four small squares of different colors to the remaining plaid diamonds, overlapping them as shown with a 1/4" gap in the center.

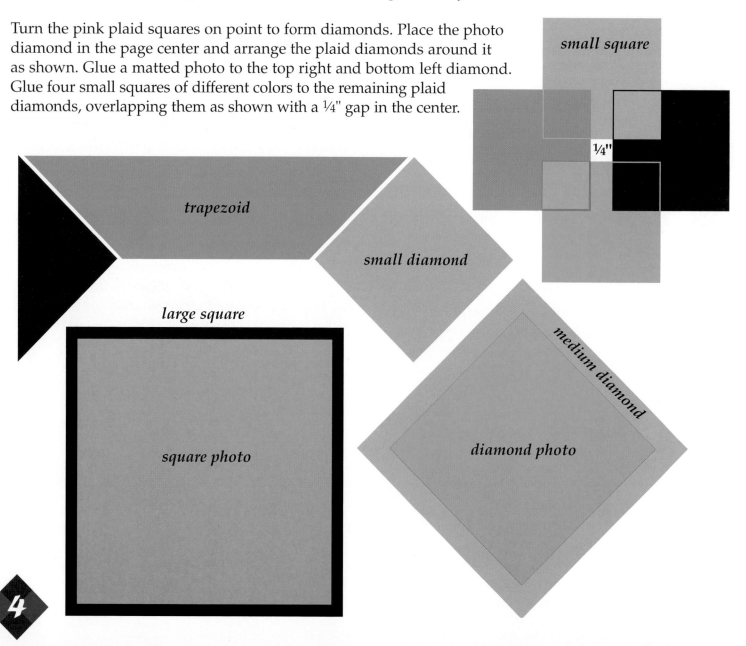

small square

1/4"

trapezoid

small diamond

large square

medium diamond

square photo

diamond photo

4

Super Star (shown inside the back cover)

◆ 12"x12" sheet of bright yellow paper
◆ 6 Punch-Outs™ from *Paper Pizazz™ Kids Punch-Outs™* (or cutouts with a childhood theme)
◆ ½" and ¼" star punches (McGill, Inc.)

Cut the following pieces:
◆ one 8" square of red dots and lines
◆ four 1¼"x8" border strips of red/blue stripe
◆ two 3¾" solid green squares
◆ four 3½" solid green squares
◆ two 3½" solid blue squares
◆ two 3" squares each of red/yellow plaid, blue with stars and blue alphabet papers; also cut 3 photos to 3" squares

Glue the 8" square to the center of the background paper and a border strip centered along each side. Glue each star square to a solid blue square and each remaining patterned square to a 3½" green square. Mat two photos on red paper and one on green, trimming ⅛" away. Mat the green-matted photo again on yellow, using patterned scissors to trim ¼" away.

Glue a red-matted photo to each 3¾" green square, positioning one at the upper left of its square and the other at the upper right, leaving two sides of each with ½" of space for journaling.

Arrange the completed squares in three rows of three as shown. Mat each Punch-Out™ on solid paper, then glue to the patterned paper squares. Decorate the page with punched blue and yellow stars.

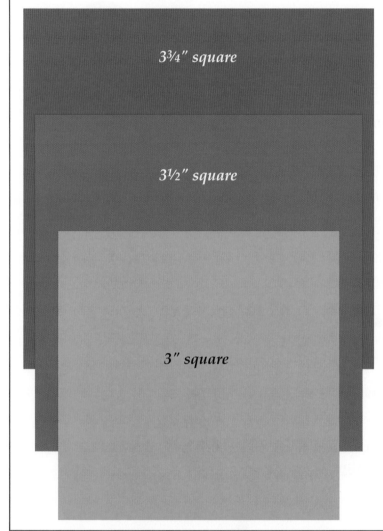

3¾" square

3½" square

3" square

8" square

border strip

Gordon (shown inside the back cover)

Cut the following pieces:
- ◆ 2 burgundy stripe photo mats
- ◆ 2 burgundy tri-dot journaling strips
- ◆ 8 burgundy tri-dot kites
- ◆ 6 burgundy stripe kites
- ◆ 3 burgundy tri-dot circles
- ◆ 4 burgundy stripe circles
- ◆ 5 burgundy tri-dot diamonds
- ◆ 5 burgundy/blue stripe diamonds
- ◆ ¼" wide burgundy tri-dot strips: two 8", two 5" long

Assemble the kites and circles into bow ties, using striped circles on dotted ties and dotted circles on striped ties.

Mat each diamond and journaling strip on solid white, trimming very close to the edge to leave a narrow white outline. Cut one diamond of each pattern in half vertically. Glue the photos and journaling strips to the photo mats as shown.

Center the 5" strips vertically, one above the other, on the background sheet. Glue one 8" strip horizontally 2¼" from the top edge of the paper and the other the same distance above the bottom. Glue a matted photo to each side, ¾" from the strips. Glue a tri-dot bow tie to the center, overlapping the photos. Glue the remaining bow ties, diamonds and diamond halves as shown.

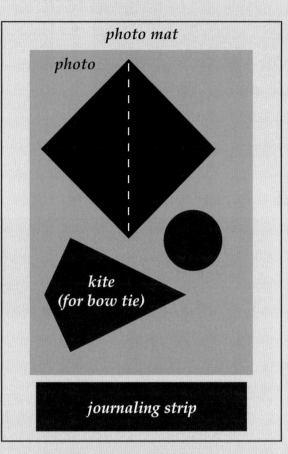

photo mat

photo

kite
(for bow tie)

journaling strip

Riding Horseback at Yamhill (shown inside the back cover)

- ◆ ³⁄₁₆" star punch (Marvy® Uchida)

Cut the following pieces:
- ◆ 3 large squares of blue with stars
- ◆ 3 large squares of blue mini-dot
- ◆ 3 large squares of rust mini-dot
- ◆ 3 large and 9 small triangles of rust mini-dot
- ◆ 3 large and 9 small triangles of country hearts
- ◆ 6 diamonds of blue with stars
- ◆ 6 diamonds of blue mini-dot
- ◆ 7 small squares of blue mini-dot
- ◆ 5 photos, 1 cream solid journaling square to match the photo square

On each large blue stars square, glue six small triangles in a row, alternating patterns as shown. Place a rust and a hearts large triangle together to form a square; repeat twice. Glue four diamonds in an X on each of these squares, alternating patterns. Glue a small square to the center of each X.

Glue the journaling square to the center of a large rust mini-dot square. Glue a small square to each corner. Glue the photos to the remaining large squares, referring to the page illustration for placement. Glue the squares to the dots and checks background sheet as shown.

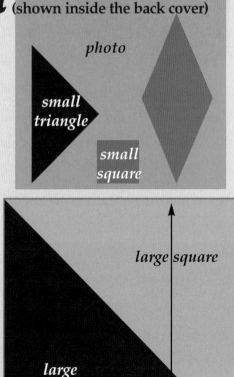

photo

small
triangle

small
square

large square

large
triangle

6

Julia's Third Birthday! (shown inside the back cover)

Cut the following pieces:

◆ 1 large and 2 small squares of rainbow stripe
◆ 4 corner triangles of rainbow stripe (stripes parallel to the long side)
◆ 2 large trapezoids of red candles
◆ 4 medium trapezoids of "Happy Birthday" (lettering parallel to the long side)
◆ 1 small square of solid yellow   ◆ 2 circles of solid green
◆ 3 square diamonds of solid red   ◆ 6 long diamonds of solid red
◆ 2 ribbon strips of solid red   ◆ 1 small journaling trapezoid of solid red
◆ 1 photo to fit the gray square (or any measurement under 4" in the longest dimension)

Glue a triangle in each corner of the blue lines & dots background paper. Glue a "Birthday" trapezoid just inside each triangle. Glue a candle trapezoid on each side and the journaling trapezoid at the bottom. Glue the large striped square in the center. Glue a ribbon strip across the center in each direction. Glue the long diamonds fanned across the top of the vertical strip to form a bow. Mat the photo on yellow, trim 1/8" away with patterned scissors and glue to the package center. Glue the square diamonds evenly spaced in the area below the package; glue the green circles between the diamonds. Glue a small striped square to each outside diamond. Turn the small yellow square on point to form a diamond and glue to the center diamond for the date.

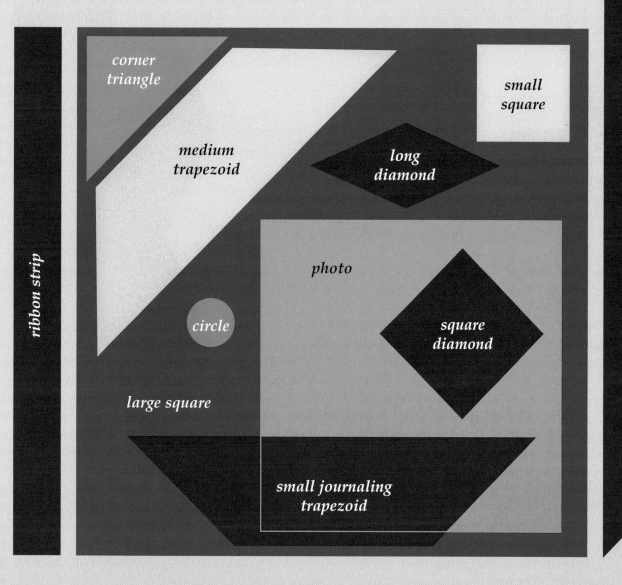

December 1996 (shown inside the back cover)

◆ ½" tree, ¾" bow punches (McGill, Inc.)

Cut the following pieces:

◆ 2 top/bottom shapes of red plaid
◆ 2 large and 4 small circles of red tri-dot
◆ 16 small diamonds of red with trees
◆ 1 photo mat of red solid

◆ 2 side shapes of holly
◆ 16 kites of red tri-dot
◆ 2 large diamonds of red plaid
◆ 1 photo to fit the gray square

Mat the two red plaid diamonds on solid red, trimming ¹⁄₁₆" away. Glue a plaid top/bottom shape to the center of the background page with the long straight edge aligned with the top page edge. Repeat at the center bottom. Glue a holly shape to the center of each side. Set the photo mat in the opening and slip a matted diamond under each side, positioning it to fill the notch in the holly shape. Glue in place. Glue the photo to the mat center. Glue a large circle to the center top and center bottom. Journal on these circles with a white opaque pen.

At one corner of the photo, arrange four diamonds in a cross with kites between them, filling the notches in the plaid and holly shapes. Allow the background to show around the edges of each piece. Glue in place and glue a small circle to the center. Repeat at each remaining corner of the photo. Decorate the journaling circles with green bow and tree punches as shown. Outline the shapes with a dashed line, using the white pen for the dark shapes and a red pen for the light shapes.

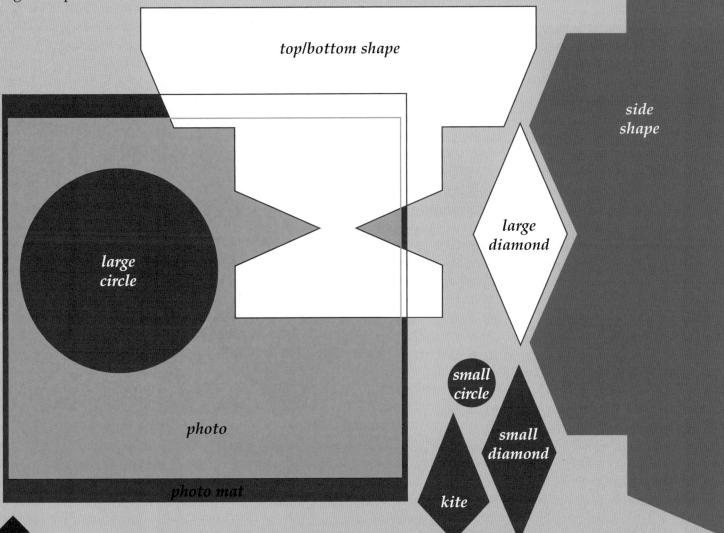

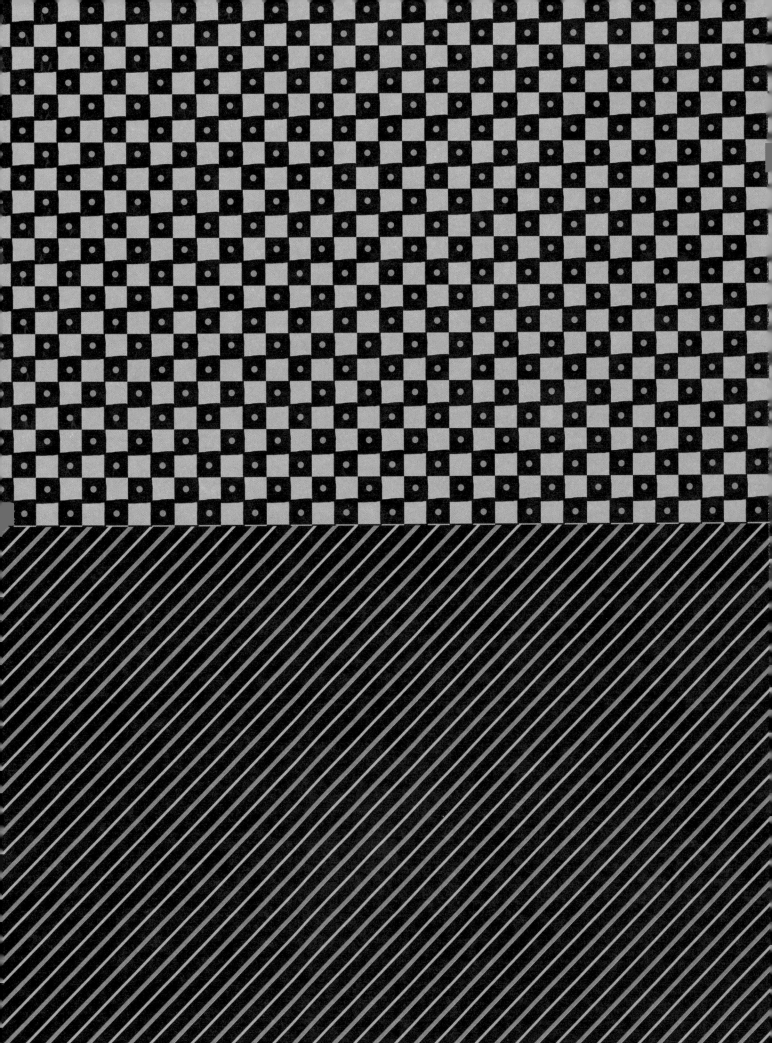

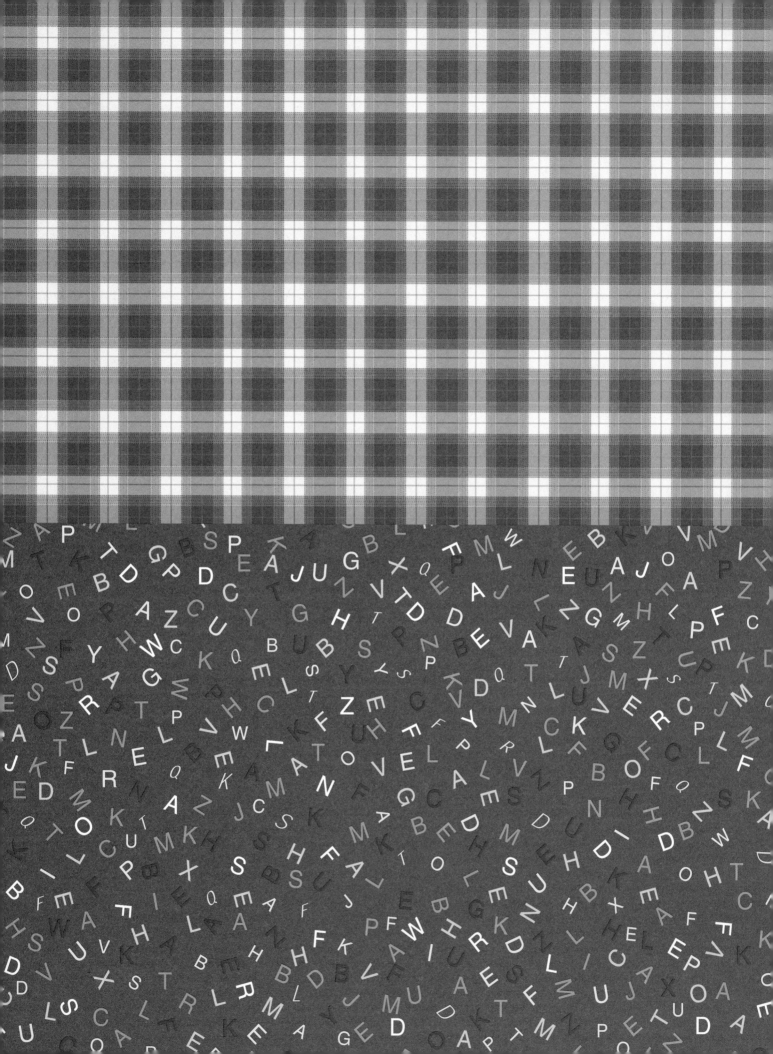